CELPIP Reading

Practice Tasks, Tips & Strategies for Success

CELPIP Reading Overview

This book offers various reading tasks that simulate the types of questions and passages found in the actual CELPIP test. The tasks are designed to assess your ability to comprehend written information and analyze it effectively. Let's take a closer look at each reading task in the CELPIP Reading Tasks:

Part 1: Reading Correspondence: 11 Questions

In this task, you are presented with a variety of short passages that resemble everyday written communication, such as emails, notes, and letters. The aim is to assess the ability to understand the main idea, identify specific details, and grasp the overall tone or purpose of the correspondence. Questions may involve identifying the writer's intention, finding specific information, or understanding implied meaning.

Part 2: Reading to Apply a Diagram: 8 Questions

This task focuses on reading passages that are accompanied by a diagram or visual representation. You must analyze the information provided in the text and use it to understand and interpret the diagram accurately. The questions may involve identifying parts of the diagram, understanding the relationship between different elements, or drawing conclusions based on the information presented.

Part 3: Reading for Information: 9 Questions

This task assesses the ability to comprehend longer passages of text, such as newspaper articles, magazine excerpts, or informative essays. You are expected to extract relevant information, understand the organization and structure of the passage, and identify key ideas, supporting details, and the writer's perspective. Questions may require summarizing the main points, making inferences, or determining the author's purpose.

Part 4: Reading for Viewpoints: 10 Questions

This task evaluates your comprehension of passages that present different viewpoints or arguments on a particular topic. The passages may be in the form of editorials, opinion pieces, or debates. The focus is on understanding the different perspectives presented, identifying the author's position, recognizing supporting evidence, and evaluating the overall argument. Test-takers may be asked to compare and contrast viewpoints, analyze the credibility of the information, or determine the main argument of the passage.

The duration of CELPIP reading tasks varies, but typically they take around **55 to 60 minutes** to complete in total on the CELPIP test.

Part 1: Reading Correspondence

Reading Part 1 of the CELPIP test assesses your ability to understand and interpret various forms of written correspondence commonly encountered in everyday life in English-speaking environments. This section evaluates your reading comprehension skills and your ability to extract information from different types of correspondence.

The Reading Correspondence section includes different types of written materials, such as:

1. Emails: You will encounter emails that you might receive or send in personal or professional settings. These emails can include invitations, requests, inquiries, or other forms of personal or business communication.

2. Instant Messages: This part will assess your understanding of short messages typically exchanged in online chats or messaging applications. The messages may involve making plans, sharing information, or engaging in casual conversations.

3. Notices: You will come across notices that are commonly found in public spaces, such as community centers, schools, or workplaces. These notices can include announcements, reminders, or instructions.

4. Classifieds and Advertisements: This category focuses on classified ads or job advertisements found in newspapers or online platforms. You will need to comprehend and extract relevant information from these advertisements.

Skills Assessed:
The Reading Correspondence section evaluates several skills related to reading and comprehension, including:

1. Understanding Main Ideas: You will be assessed on your ability to identify the main ideas and key points presented in the correspondence.

2. Interpreting Details: This part tests your comprehension of specific details, such as dates, times, locations, prices, or other factual information mentioned in the correspondence.

3. Inference and Deduction: You will need to make reasonable inferences and deductions based on the information provided in the correspondence.

4. Vocabulary and Contextual Understanding: Your understanding of vocabulary in context will be assessed. You need to grasp the meaning of words or phrases based on the surrounding text.

5. Purpose and Tone: This section evaluates your ability to identify the purpose and tone of the correspondence, whether it is informative, persuasive, formal, or informal.

Question Format:
For each item in the Reading Correspondence section, you will encounter a question or an incomplete statement. You will have to choose the most appropriate option from the given multiple-choice responses. The options can include completing a sentence, selecting a suitable title, identifying the purpose, or matching a statement with a specific correspondence.

Preparation Tips:
To perform well in the CELPIP Reading Part 1: Reading Correspondence, consider the following tips:

1. Enhance Vocabulary: Work on expanding your vocabulary to understand a wide range of words and expressions used in different types of correspondence.

2. Practice Skimming and Scanning: Develop your ability to quickly scan through the correspondence to find relevant information and identify main ideas.

3. Familiarize Yourself with Different Formats: Get acquainted with various types of correspondence, such as emails, instant messages, notices, and advertisements, to become comfortable with their structures and purposes.

4. Practice Time Management: Allocate sufficient time for each question and section. Practicing under timed conditions will help you manage your time effectively during the actual test.

5. Read Widely: Engage in extensive reading of English materials, such as newspapers, magazines, online articles, and books. This will improve your reading speed, comprehension, and overall language skills.

Remember, regular practice, exposure to different types of correspondence, and a solid understanding of the question format will greatly contribute to your success in the CELPIP Reading Part 1.

10 Tips for Part 1: Reading Correspondence

Here are ten tips and examples to help you pass the CELPIP Reading Part 1: Reading Correspondence:

1. Read the Instructions Carefully: Pay close attention to the instructions provided for each question. Understand what is being asked before attempting to answer.

Example: "Choose the option that best completes the sentence" or "Select the title that best describes the passage."

2. Skim the Correspondence: Quickly scan through the correspondence to get a general understanding of the content and to identify any headings, subheadings, or important keywords.

Example: Skim through an email to identify phrases like "meeting details" or "important announcement."

3. Highlight Keywords: Once you have skimmed the correspondence, go back and highlight or underline keywords that are relevant to the question being asked. This will help you focus on the key information while answering.

Example: Highlight words like "date," "time," or "location" when searching for specific details.

4. Identify the Purpose and Tone: Pay attention to the purpose and tone of the correspondence, as this can help you determine the appropriate answer.

Example: Identify whether an email is formal or informal, or whether a notice is meant to inform or persuade.

5. Understand the Context: Consider the context in which the correspondence is written. This will help you make accurate inferences and deductions.

Example: If an email is discussing a project deadline, consider the context of a workplace setting and the implications of meeting the deadline.

6. Eliminate Incorrect Options: If you are unsure about an answer, try to eliminate any obviously incorrect options. This increases your chances of selecting the correct answer.

Example: If the correspondence is about a social event, eliminate options that relate to a work meeting.

7. Pay Attention to Quantitative Information: Be mindful of numerical or quantitative information mentioned in the correspondence, such as dates, times, prices, or quantities. These details are often essential to answer the questions accurately.

Example: If the question asks for the date of an event, pay attention to any specific date mentioned in the correspondence.

8. Practice Time Management: Since the CELPIP test is time-limited, it's crucial to manage your time effectively. Allocate a specific amount of time for each question, and move on if you're struggling with a particular item.

Example: Set a time limit of 1 minute and 30 seconds per question to ensure you have enough time to answer all the items.

9. Review Your Answers: If time permits, review your answers before submitting the test. Double-check for any errors or potential improvements.

Example: Review your selected options for each question to ensure they are the best choices based on the information provided.

10. Practice with Sample Tests: Familiarize yourself with the format and types of questions by practicing with sample tests. This will help you become comfortable with the test structure and improve your overall performance.

Example: Use practice materials provided by CELPIP or seek out additional resources that offer sample Reading Correspondence sections.

By implementing these tips and practicing regularly, you can improve your performance in the CELPIP Reading Part 1: Reading Correspondence section.

Practice 1: Part 1: Reading Correspondence

Read the following message:

"Hi Tom,

I hope this email finds you well. It's been quite a while since we last caught up, and I have some exciting news to share with you. I've recently been offered a job opportunity in London, and I have accepted it. I'm both nervous and thrilled about this new chapter in my life.

The position is with a renowned advertising agency in the heart of the city. They specialize in digital marketing and have worked on some incredible campaigns. I'm looking forward to being part of such a creative and dynamic team. The role itself is quite challenging, but I believe it will push me to grow professionally.

The move to London will be a big change for me. I'll be leaving behind my family and friends here in New York. However, I see it as a chance for personal growth and new experiences. London is such a vibrant city, and I can't wait to explore its rich history and cultural scene.

I wanted to reach out and see if you would be available to meet up before I leave. It would be great to catch up and have one last get-together. Let me know what works for you, and we can make the necessary arrangements.

Thanks, Tom! I appreciate your support and friendship over the years. I'll keep you updated on my London adventures.

Take care,
Sara"

Questions for Reading Passage:

1. What is the purpose of Sara's email?
a) To invite Tom to a farewell party.

b) To inform Tom about her new job opportunity in London.

c) To ask for Tom's opinion on moving to London.

2. How does Sara feel about the job opportunity in London?

a) She is uncertain.

b) She is nervous and thrilled.

c) She is disappointed.

3. Which industry is Sara's new job in?

a) Advertising.

b) Finance.

c) Education.

4. What does Sara look forward to in London?

a) Exploring the city's history and culture.

b) Being closer to her family and friends.

c) Advancing her career in finance.

5. How does Sara view the move to London?

a) A chance for personal growth and new experiences.

b) A difficult decision she regrets.

c) An opportunity to be closer to her family.

6. What does Sara want to do with Tom before she leaves?

a) Have a farewell party.

b) Plan a trip to London.

c) Meet up for a final get-together.

Read the following announcement:

"Attention all students!

We are excited to announce the launch of our new mentorship program at XYZ University. The program aims to provide guidance and support to students as they navigate their academic journey and prepare for their future careers.

As a mentee, you will be paired with a knowledgeable and experienced mentor who will share valuable insights, offer career advice, and help you develop important skills. Your mentor will be there to answer your questions, provide feedback on your progress, and assist you in setting and achieving your academic and professional goals.

This program offers a unique opportunity for networking and building connections within your chosen field. Your mentor can introduce you to industry professionals, provide recommendations, and open doors to internships and job opportunities.

To participate in the mentorship program, simply fill out the application form available on our university website. We will carefully match you with a mentor based on your academic interests and career aspirations.

Don't miss out on this valuable opportunity to enhance your university experience and set yourself up for success. Apply now and unlock the benefits of mentorship!"

Questions for Reading Passage 2:

7. What is the main purpose of the announcement?
a)To introduce a new mentorship program at XYZ University.
b) To promote a networking event for students.
c) To inform students about changes in the university curriculum.

8. What can students expect from the mentorship program?
a) Financial support for their academic endeavors.
b) Guidance and support from experienced mentors.
c) Access to exclusive internships.

9. How can students apply for the mentorship program?
a) By attending an information session.
b) By contacting the university administration directly.
c) By filling out an application form on the university website.

10. What benefits can students gain from the mentorship program?

a) Valuable insights and career advice.
b) A chance to meet industry professionals.
c) Access to scholarships.

11. What is the purpose of matching students with mentors?
a) To build connections within the university community.
b) To provide recommendations for job opportunities.
c) To ensure a suitable mentor-mentee relationship based on interests and aspirations.

Correct Answers:

1) b) To inform Tom about her new job opportunity in London.
2) b) She is nervous and thrilled.
3) a) Advertising.
4) a) Exploring the city's history and culture.
5) a) A chance for personal growth and new experiences.
6) c) Meet up for a final get-together.
7) a) To introduce a new mentorship program at XYZ University.
8) b) Guidance and support from experienced mentors.
9) c) By filling out an application form on the university website.
10) a) Valuable insights and career advice.
11) c) To ensure a suitable mentor-mentee relationship based on interests and aspirations.

Practice 2: Part 1: Reading Correspondence

Read the following message:

"Dear Alex,

I hope this email finds you well. I wanted to share some exciting news with you. After years of hard work and dedication, I have been accepted into the medical school of my dreams. I am overjoyed and incredibly grateful for this opportunity.

The medical school is renowned for its rigorous curriculum and cutting-edge research facilities. I am confident that the education and training I will receive there will prepare me for a successful career in medicine. It has always been my passion to make a positive impact on people's lives through healthcare, and this acceptance brings me one step closer to achieving that goal.

The program is set to begin in September, which means I will be moving to the city where the medical school is located. It's an exciting but also daunting prospect. Leaving my family and friends behind is bittersweet, but I know that pursuing this path is the right decision for me.

Before I leave, I would love to spend some time with you and catch up. It has been too long since we last saw each other. Perhaps we can plan a weekend getaway or even just a dinner together. Let me know what works for you, and we can make the necessary arrangements.

Thank you for always being a supportive friend. I look forward to sharing more updates about my journey in medical school.

Take care,
Emma"

Questions for Reading Passage:

1. What is the purpose of Emma's email?

a) To invite Alex to a celebratory party.
b) To inform Alex about her acceptance into medical school.
c) To request financial assistance for her education.

2. How does Emma feel about being accepted into medical school?
a) She is uncertain.
b) She is overjoyed and grateful.
c) She is disappointed.

3. What is the reputation of the medical school Emma got accepted into?
a) It is known for its rigorous curriculum and research facilities.
b) It is known for its arts and humanities programs.
c) It is known for its sports teams.

4. What is Emma's ultimate goal in pursuing medicine?
a) To become a renowned researcher.
b) To make a positive impact on people's lives through healthcare.
c) To secure a high-paying job.

5. How does Emma feel about leaving her family and friends?
a) She is excited and ready for a fresh start.
b) She is bittersweet about leaving them behind.
c) She is reluctant to pursue her dreams.

6. What does Emma want to do with Alex before she leaves?
a) Plan a celebratory party.
b) Spend quality time together and catch up.
c) Ask for financial support for her education.

Read the following announcement:

"Attention all employees!

We are pleased to announce the launch of our wellness program at our company. The program aims to promote a healthier lifestyle among our employees and provide resources for physical and mental well-being.

The wellness program offers various activities and initiatives, including yoga classes, fitness challenges, and mindfulness workshops. These activities are designed to help reduce stress, improve overall fitness levels, and enhance work-life balance. Additionally, we have partnered with local gyms and wellness centers to offer discounted memberships exclusively for our employees.

In line with our commitment to employee well-being, we have also established a confidential counseling service. This service provides professional support for any personal or work-related issues employees may face. We believe that mental health is as important as physical health, and we want to ensure a supportive and nurturing work environment.

Participation in the wellness program is voluntary, and we encourage all employees to take advantage of the resources and activities available. We believe that investing in the well-being of our employees

will not only improve individual health but also enhance productivity and job satisfaction.

Further details about the wellness program, including the schedule of activities and how to sign up, will be shared with all employees in the coming weeks. We look forward to your active participation in this exciting initiative.

Stay well,
The HR Team"

Questions for Reading Passage:

7. What is the purpose of the announcement?
a) To introduce a new wellness program at the company.
b) To announce a change in the company's management.
c) To inform employees about upcoming promotions.

8. What activities are included in the wellness program?
a) Leadership training and team-building exercises.
b) Yoga classes, fitness challenges, and mindfulness workshops.
c) Sales competitions and customer service training.

9. What are the benefits of participating in the wellness program?
a) Access to discounted gym memberships.
b) Improved work-life balance and reduced stress.
c) Higher salary and job promotions.

10. Why did the company establish a confidential counseling service?
a) To help employees with personal and work-related issues.
b) To cut costs and reduce employee benefits.
c) To enforce strict disciplinary actions.

11. What is the company's belief regarding employee well-being?
a) Mental health is more important than physical health.
b) Employee well-being has no impact on job satisfaction.
c) Investing in employee well-being improves productivity and job satisfaction.

Correct Answers:

1) b) To inform Alex about her acceptance into medical school.
2) b) She is overjoyed and grateful.
3) a) It is known for its rigorous curriculum and research facilities.
4) b) To make a positive impact on people's lives through healthcare.
5) b) She is bittersweet about leaving them behind.
6) b) Spend quality time together and catch up.
7) a) To introduce a new wellness program at the company.
8) b) Yoga classes, fitness challenges, and mindfulness workshops.
9) b) Improved work-life balance and reduced stress.
10) a) To help employees with personal and work-related issues.
11) c) Investing in employee well-being improves productivity and job satisfaction.

Practice 3: Part 1: Reading Correspondence

Read the following message:

"The Importance of Sustainable Living

Sustainable living has become an increasingly important topic in today's world. It refers to a lifestyle that aims to minimize our impact on the environment and preserve natural resources for future generations. Adopting sustainable practices is crucial for mitigating climate change, reducing pollution, and promoting ecological balance.

One of the key aspects of sustainable living is energy conservation. By using energy-efficient appliances, practicing smart energy consumption habits, and utilizing renewable energy sources such as solar power, individuals can significantly reduce their carbon footprint. This not only helps combat climate change but also leads to long-term cost savings.

Another essential component of sustainable living is waste reduction and recycling. Instead of sending waste to landfills, individuals can opt for recycling programs and composting. This reduces the amount of waste that ends up in landfills and contributes to the depletion of natural resources. Additionally, reducing consumption and choosing products with minimal packaging can further minimize waste generation.

Water conservation is another critical aspect of sustainable living. With water scarcity becoming a global concern, it is vital to use water efficiently and avoid unnecessary wastage. Simple actions like fixing leaks, using low-flow fixtures, and practicing responsible irrigation can go a long way in preserving this precious resource.

Sustainable living also encompasses sustainable transportation. By reducing reliance on private cars and opting for public transportation, carpooling, cycling, or walking, individuals can reduce greenhouse gas emissions and promote cleaner air quality in cities. Additionally, choosing fuel-efficient vehicles or electric cars can further contribute to a sustainable transportation system.

In conclusion, sustainable living is essential for creating a greener and healthier planet. It requires a collective effort from individuals, communities, and governments to adopt sustainable practices in various aspects of life. By embracing sustainable living, we can ensure a brighter future for generations to come."

Questions for Reading Passage:

1. What is the main focus of sustainable living?
a) Minimizing impact on the environment and preserving resources.
b) Maximizing energy consumption for personal benefit.
c) Promoting technological advancements without considering the environment.

2. How can individuals reduce their carbon footprint?
a) By using energy-efficient appliances and renewable energy sources.
b) By consuming more energy to support economic growth.
c) By increasing waste production and recycling.

3. What are the benefits of waste reduction and recycling?
a) Increased landfill capacity and resource depletion.
b) Reduced waste in landfills and preservation of resources.
c) Higher waste generation and pollution.

4. Why is water conservation important?
a) To increase water usage and availability.
b) To ensure water scarcity becomes a global concern.
c) To preserve water resources and combat scarcity.

5. What actions can individuals take to conserve water?
a) Fixing leaks, using low-flow fixtures, and practicing responsible irrigation.

b) Increasing water consumption for personal needs.
c) Ignoring water wastage and relying on natural replenishment.

6. How can sustainable transportation be achieved?
a) By relying solely on private cars and avoiding public transportation.
b) By reducing greenhouse gas emissions and promoting cleaner air quality.
c) By increasing reliance on fuel-inefficient vehicles.

Read the following news excerpt:

"New Environmental Regulations for Industrial Plants

The government has recently introduced stricter environmental regulations for industrial plants. The aim is to reduce pollution, protect natural resources, and ensure a healthier environment for communities living near these facilities.

Under the new regulations, industrial plants will be required to install advanced air pollution control systems to minimize emissions. This includes the use of effective filtration systems, monitoring equipment, and adherence to emission limits set by environmental agencies.

Additionally, industrial plants will need to implement wastewater treatment processes to prevent the contamination

of water bodies. This involves treating effluents before releasing them into rivers or oceans, reducing the discharge of harmful substances and pollutants.

To promote energy efficiency, the regulations also mandate the adoption of energy management systems in industrial plants. This includes the implementation of energy-saving measures, regular energy audits, and the use of energy-efficient technologies.

Furthermore, the government will be conducting regular

inspections and monitoring of industrial plants to ensure compliance with the new regulations. Non-compliance may result in fines, penalties, or even the suspension of operations.

These new environmental regulations reflect the government's commitment to sustainable development and environmental stewardship. By enforcing stricter standards, they aim to create a cleaner and safer environment for all."

Questions for Reading Passage:

7. What is the purpose of the new environmental regulations?
a) To promote pollution and harm natural resources.
b) To protect the environment and reduce pollution from industrial plants.
c) To encourage industrial plants to disregard environmental concerns.

8. What measures are required to minimize emissions from industrial plants?
a) Installation of air pollution control systems and adherence to emission limits.
b) Ignoring emissions and focusing on increased production.
c) Encouraging industrial plants to increase pollution levels.

9. What is the purpose of implementing wastewater treatment processes?
a) To increase the contamination of water bodies.
b) To prevent pollution and protect water bodies from harmful substances.
c) To encourage the discharge of untreated effluents.

10. What is the goal of adopting energy management systems in industrial plants?
a) To promote energy wastage and increase emissions.
b) To encourage energy-saving measures and improve energy efficiency.
c) To disregard energy consumption and focus on maximizing

production.

11. What actions will the government take to ensure compliance with the new regulations?
a) Conduct regular inspections and monitoring of industrial plants.
b) Encourage non-compliance with the regulations.
c) Reward industrial plants for disregarding environmental standards.

Correct Answers:

1) a) Minimizing impact on the environment and preserving resources.
2) a) By using energy-efficient appliances and renewable energy sources.
3) b) Reduced waste in landfills and preservation of resources.
4) c) To preserve water resources and combat scarcity.
5) a) Fixing leaks, using low-flow fixtures, and practicing responsible irrigation.
6) b) By reducing greenhouse gas emissions and promoting cleaner air quality.
7) b) To protect the environment and reduce pollution from industrial plants.
8) a) Installation of air pollution control systems and adherence to emission limits.
9) b) To prevent pollution and protect water bodies from harmful substances.
10) b) To encourage energy-saving measures and improve energy efficiency.
11) a) Conduct regular inspections and monitoring of industrial plants.

Practice 4: Part 1: Reading Correspondence

Read the following article:

"The Benefits of Outdoor Exercise

Exercise is essential for maintaining a healthy lifestyle, and engaging in outdoor physical activities brings a range of benefits. While indoor workouts have their advantages, outdoor exercise offers unique advantages that contribute to physical and mental well-being.

One of the primary benefits of outdoor exercise is exposure to natural sunlight. Sunlight is a natural source of vitamin D, which plays a crucial role in bone health and overall immune function. Spending time outdoors allows the body to absorb sunlight and produce vitamin D, reducing the risk of deficiencies.

Outdoor exercise also provides an opportunity to connect with nature. Being surrounded by green spaces, trees, and fresh air can have a calming effect on the mind and reduce stress levels. Studies have shown that spending time in nature can enhance mood, boost mental clarity, and improve overall psychological well-being.

Furthermore, outdoor exercise often involves varied terrains and surfaces, which can engage different muscles and improve balance and coordination. Activities like hiking, trail running, and outdoor sports require constant adjustments to the terrain, challenging the body in new ways and promoting functional fitness.

Another advantage of outdoor exercise is the potential for social interaction. Participating in group activities, such as team sports or outdoor fitness classes, provides opportunities to meet like-minded individuals, build friendships, and foster a sense of community. Social support and connection have been linked to improved motivation and adherence to an exercise routine.

Lastly, outdoor exercise offers a break from the monotony of indoor settings. Being in nature stimulates the senses and provides a refreshing change of scenery. This can enhance enjoyment and make workouts feel less like a chore, leading to increased motivation and consistency in physical activity.

In conclusion, incorporating outdoor exercise into one's fitness routine can bring numerous benefits. From exposure to natural sunlight and connection with nature to varied terrains and social interaction, outdoor exercise offers a holistic approach to physical and mental well-being."

Questions for Reading Passage:

1. What are the unique advantages of outdoor exercise?
a) Improved physical and mental well-being.
b) Enhanced indoor workout routines.
c) Increased motivation for indoor exercises.

2. What role does sunlight play in outdoor exercise?
a) It reduces the need for vitamin D production in the body.
b) It provides a natural source of vitamin D, benefiting bone health and immune function.
c) It has no significant impact on the body during exercise.

3. How does spending time in nature affect mental well-being?
a) It has no effect on stress levels and mood.
b) It boosts mental clarity and reduces stress levels.
c) It only improves psychological well-being temporarily.

4. What advantage does outdoor exercise offer in terms of muscle engagement?
a) It engages the same muscles repeatedly, promoting muscle imbalances.
b) It challenges different muscles and improves balance and coordination.
c) It has no impact on muscle development.

5. How does outdoor exercise contribute to social interaction?
a) It isolates individuals from others, reducing social contact.
b) It allows for group activities and the opportunity to meet like-minded individuals.
c) It discourages social connections and friendship building.

6. How does being in nature affect the enjoyment of exercise?
a) It makes workouts feel like a chore and decreases motivation.
b) It provides a refreshing change of scenery and enhances enjoyment.
c) It has no impact on exercise enjoyment.

Read the following news excerpt:

"Benefits of Urban Parks

Urban parks play a crucial role in enhancing the quality of life for city dwellers. These green spaces offer numerous benefits that contribute to physical health, mental well-being, and community development.

One of the primary benefits of urban parks is their contribution to physical activity. These spaces provide opportunities for

various recreational activities such as walking, jogging, cycling, and team sports. Regular physical activity in urban parks can help combat sedentary lifestyles, promote cardiovascular health, and reduce the risk of chronic diseases.

Urban parks also offer a respite from the hustle and bustle of city life. They provide an escape from the concrete jungle and offer a peaceful environment for relaxation and stress reduction. Spending time in green spaces has been linked to improved mental health, reduced anxiety and depression, and enhanced overall well-being.

Furthermore, urban parks serve as gathering places for communities. They bring people from diverse backgrounds together, promoting social cohesion and interaction. Parks provide spaces for socializing, picnics, community events, and cultural activities. These interactions foster a sense of belonging, strengthen social ties, and create a sense of community pride.

Additionally, urban parks contribute to environmental sustainability. They act as green lungs in cities, absorbing carbon dioxide and releasing oxygen, thereby improving air quality. Parks also serve as habitats for various species of plants and animals, supporting biodiversity and preserving ecological balance.

In conclusion, urban parks offer a range of benefits, including opportunities for physical activity, mental well-being, community building, and environmental sustainability. They are invaluable assets for cities and should be preserved and further developed to enhance the overall quality of urban life."

Questions for Reading Passage:

7. What benefits do urban parks provide for physical health?
a) They increase the risk of chronic diseases.
b) They promote cardiovascular health and combat sedentary lifestyles.
c) They have no impact on physical well-being.

8. How do urban parks contribute to mental well-being?
a) They exacerbate anxiety and depression.
b) They provide a peaceful environment for relaxation and stress reduction.
c) They have no effect on mental health.

9. What role do urban parks play in community development?
a) They isolate individuals and hinder social interaction.
b) They bring diverse communities together and promote social cohesion.
c) They have no impact on community bonds.

10. How do urban parks contribute to environmental sustainability?

a) They have no impact on air quality.
b) They absorb carbon dioxide and release oxygen, improving air quality.
c) They harm biodiversity and disrupt ecological balance.

11. What is the overall conclusion about the importance of urban parks?
a) They have no significance in enhancing urban life.
b) They provide opportunities for physical activity, mental well-being, community building, and environmental sustainability.
c) They are unnecessary and should be eliminated from cities.

Correct Answers:

1) a) Improved physical and mental well-being.
2) b) It provides a natural source of vitamin D, benefiting bone health and immune function.
3) b) It boosts mental clarity and reduces stress levels.
4) b) It challenges different muscles and improves balance and coordination.
5) b) It allows for group activities and the opportunity to meet like-minded individuals.
6) b) It provides a refreshing change of scenery and enhances enjoyment.
7) b) They promote cardiovascular health and combat sedentary lifestyles.
8) b) They provide a peaceful environment for relaxation and stress reduction.
9) b) They bring diverse communities together and promote social cohesion.
10) b) They absorb carbon dioxide and release oxygen, improving air quality.
11) b) They provide opportunities for physical activity, mental well-being, community building, and environmental sustainability.

Part 2: Reading to Apply a Diagram

CELPIP Reading Part 2 is a section of the CELPIP test that assesses your ability to understand and analyze information presented in the form of diagrams, charts, graphs, and tables. In this section, you will be required to read a passage and use the provided diagram to answer a series of questions.

Here's a detailed overview of the CELPIP Reading Part 2 section:

Format:
- You will be given a passage of text that provides information on a specific topic, such as a process, a system, or a set of data.
- Accompanying the passage, there will be a diagram, which could be a flowchart, a map, a diagram of a machine, or any other visual representation relevant to the topic.
- The questions will require you to apply your understanding of the information in the passage to interpret and analyze the diagram.

Objective:
The main objective of this section is to assess your ability to:
1. Understand the relationship between textual information and visual representations.
2. Extract key information from the passage and map it onto the diagram.
3. Identify and interpret different elements and components within the diagram.
4. Make inferences and draw conclusions based on the information provided.

Question Types:
The questions in this section can vary but generally fall into the following categories:
1. Labeling: You may be asked to label specific parts or components on the diagram using information from the passage.
2. Matching: You may be required to match descriptions or

statements from the passage with corresponding elements or sections in the diagram.

3. Sequencing: You might need to determine the correct order or sequence of events depicted in the diagram based on the information in the passage.

4. Identifying Relationships: You could be asked to identify relationships, connections, or dependencies between different elements in the diagram.

5. Drawing Conclusions: You may need to draw conclusions or make inferences based on the information presented in both the passage and the diagram.

Strategies:

To perform well in CELPIP Reading Part 2, consider the following strategies:

1. Read the passage carefully: Understand the main ideas, details, and any instructions or explanations provided in the passage.

2. Study the diagram: Pay attention to the labels, arrows, symbols, and any other visual cues that can help you understand the diagram's structure and purpose.

3. Analyze the relationship: Identify how the information in the passage relates to the diagram. Look for keywords, phrases, or numbers that can help you connect the two.

4. Read the questions: Read each question carefully, paying attention to what it asks for and the specific details mentioned. Take note of any keywords or cues that can guide you.

5. Cross-reference: Compare the information in the passage with the diagram and vice versa. Look for matches, patterns, or discrepancies that can help you answer the questions accurately.

6. Eliminate options: If you're unsure about an answer, use the process of elimination by ruling out options that don't align with the information provided in the passage or diagram.

7. Manage your time: Allocate time wisely for reading, analyzing, and answering the questions. Don't spend too much time on a single question; move on and come back later if needed.

Remember, practice is key to improving your performance in CELPIP Reading Part 2. Familiarize yourself with different types of diagrams and their associated question formats. Work on enhancing your ability to understand visual representations and connect them with textual information.

10 Tips for Part 2: Reading to Apply a Diagram

Here are 10 tips and examples to help you pass CELPIP Reading Part 2:

1. Read the passage carefully: Pay close attention to the details, instructions, and main ideas presented in the passage. Understand the context before moving on to the diagram.

Example: If the passage describes a process for manufacturing a product, note the key steps and factors mentioned, such as materials, equipment, or quality control measures.

2. Study the diagram: Familiarize yourself with the diagram provided. Look for labels, arrows, symbols, or any visual cues that can help you understand the structure and purpose of the diagram.

Example: If the diagram is a flowchart illustrating the steps of a scientific experiment, note the symbols used to represent different actions, variables, or measurements.

3. Identify the relationship: Analyze how the information in the passage relates to the diagram. Look for connections, dependencies, or patterns that can help you understand how the two are linked.

Example: If the passage discusses the functions and components of a computer system, the diagram might show the different hardware components and their interconnections.

4. Pay attention to labels and captions: Labels on the diagram and captions in the passage can provide valuable information. Use them to match elements, understand processes, or identify specific components.

Example: If the passage refers to "Component A" and the diagram has labeled sections, locate the corresponding label on the diagram to understand the information associated with it.

5. Look for patterns and sequences: If the diagram represents a process or a sequence of events, pay attention to the order or flow indicated. Use the information in the passage to determine the correct sequence.

Example: If the passage describes the stages of a plant's growth, the diagram might show the plant at different growth phases. Match the descriptions in the passage with the corresponding stages in the diagram.

6. Use contextual clues: Both the passage and the diagram contain valuable clues that can help you answer the questions. Pay attention to keywords, numbers, symbols, or any other cues that provide context or guide your understanding.

Example: If the passage mentions specific measurements or quantities, such as "temperature" or "time," use those clues to identify the corresponding elements or sections in the diagram.

7. Compare and contrast: Look for similarities and differences between the information in the passage and the elements in the diagram. Use these comparisons to make accurate connections and draw conclusions.

Example: If the passage discusses the advantages and disadvantages of different transportation modes, the diagram might show the environmental impact or cost associated with each mode.

8. Eliminate incorrect options: If you're unsure about an answer, use the process of elimination. Cross-reference the passage and the diagram to eliminate options that do not align with the information provided.

Example: If a question asks you to match a description with a specific element in the diagram, eliminate options that do not share the same characteristics or properties described in the passage.

9. Practice with different diagram types: Familiarize yourself with various diagram formats, such as flowcharts, maps, graphs, or diagrams of machinery. Work on understanding how to interpret each type effectively.

Example: Practice analyzing flowcharts that represent processes, maps that show geographical information, or graphs that display statistical data.

10. Manage your time effectively: Time management is crucial in the CELPIP exam. Allocate sufficient time to read the passage, analyze the diagram, and answer the questions. Avoid spending too much time on a single question.

Example: Set a time limit for each question, and if you find yourself struggling, move on to the next question and come back later if time permits.

Remember, these tips are meant to guide you in approaching CELPIP Reading Part 2. Regular practice and exposure to different diagram types will enhance your skills and confidence in analyzing and applying information from diagrams.

Practice 1: Part 2: Reading to Apply a Diagram

Read the following advertisement:

"Welcome to Paradise Beach Resort!
Escape to our tropical oasis and experience the ultimate vacation getaway.

1. Ocean View Suite:
- Stunning views of the turquoise ocean
- Private balcony
- King-sized bed
- Mini-fridge and coffee maker
- Price: $300 per night

2. Poolside Villa:
- Direct access to the pool
- Spacious patio with lounge chairs
- Two bedrooms and a living room
- Fully equipped kitchen
- Price: $450 per night

3. Beach Bungalow:
- Steps away from the beach
- Hammocks and beach chairs
- One bedroom with a cozy queen-sized bed
- Outdoor shower
- Price: $250 per night

4. Family Cabana:
- Perfect for families with kids
- Play area with swings and slides
- Two bedrooms and a loft
- Complimentary breakfast
- Price: $400 per night"

Read the following email message about the advertisement. Complete the email by filling in the blanks. Select the best

choice:

"Hi Sarah,

I hope this email finds you well. I came across an amazing advertisement for a vacation spot, and I thought of you and your family. We all deserve a break, don't we?

This resort seems like a dream! The *1.(Ocean View Suite/Poolside Villa/Beach Bungalow/Family Cabana)* offers breathtaking views of the ocean, and it even has a private balcony. I can already imagine sipping a cup of coffee while gazing at the waves. However, the *2.(Poolside Villa/Beach Bungalow/Family Cabana/Ocean View Suite)* seems more suitable for us because of the spacious patio and direct access to the pool. Our kids would have a blast!

The prices are quite reasonable, with the *3.($300 per night/$450 per night/$250 per night/$400 per night)* being the most affordable option. I think it's a great deal considering the amenities and the location. Imagine waking up to the sound of crashing waves or spending lazy afternoons lounging in the hammocks.

Let me know what you think. I'm open to other suggestions too, if you have any. We all deserve a memorable vacation.

Take care,
Emily"

Choose the best option:

4. Sarah and Emily *(are colleagues/are childhood friends/are siblings/are neighbors)*
5. The main purpose of the trip is *(to celebrate a birthday/to enjoy a romantic getaway/to spend quality time with family/to attend a business conference)*
6. Emily seems *(excited and enthusiastic/cautious and uncertain/indifferent and disinterested/hesitant and skeptical)*
7.The resort mentioned in the email is appealing to Sarah and Emily because they are looking for a vacation that offers

(luxurious accommodations/fun activities for kids/a serene beach experience/a budget-friendly option).

8. Based on Emily's email, it can be inferred that Sarah and Emily are *(close friends/co-workers/relatives/neighbors).*

Answer Key:

1. Ocean View Suite.
2. Poolside Villa.
3. $250 per night.
4. Childhood friends.
5. To spend quality time with family.
6. Excited and enthusiastic.
7. Fun activities for kids.
8. Close friends.

Practice 2: Part 2: Reading to Apply a Diagram

Read the following diagram:

1. Restaurant A:
- Fine dining experience
- Extensive wine selection
- Chef's tasting menu available
- Price: $150 per person
- Duration: Approximately 3 hours

2. Restaurant B:
- Casual atmosphere
- Family-friendly menu options
- Outdoor seating available
- Price: $50 per person
- Duration: 1-2 hours

3. Restaurant C:
- Ethnic cuisine
- Vegan and gluten-free options
- Live music on weekends
- Price: $80 per person
- Duration: 2-3 hours

4. Restaurant D:
- Trendy fusion cuisine
- Craft cocktails and mixology bar
- Rooftop dining with city views
- Price: $120 per person
- Duration: 2 hours

Read the following email message about the diagram. Complete the email by filling in the blanks. Select the best choice for questions 1 to 5:

Subject: Dinner Plans
To: Alex Thompson <alexthompson@email.com>

From: Lisa Roberts <lisaroberts@email.com>

Hi Alex,

I hope you're doing well. I wanted to discuss our dinner plans for this weekend. I've found some interesting options in town, and I think we can have a wonderful dining experience. Let's go over the details. Restaurant A offers an upscale fine dining experience with an extensive wine selection. They even have a chef's tasting menu if we're feeling adventurous. However, the price is 1.(quite high/affordable/well worth it/a bit expensive) for some. On the other hand, Restaurant B has a more casual atmosphere and is family-friendly. It could be a good option if we're looking for a laid-back meal. The price is reasonable, and we can expect to spend around 2.(an hour/two to three hours/half a day/a full day) there. Another choice is Restaurant C, which specializes in ethnic cuisine and offers vegan and gluten-free options. They also have live music on weekends, which could add to the ambiance. The price is 3.(quite high/affordable/well worth it/a bit expensive) compared to some other options. Lastly, Restaurant D combines trendy fusion cuisine with a craft cocktails and mixology bar. It's known for its rooftop dining area with stunning city views. The price is 4.(a bit steep/affordable/a bargain/expensive) but could be worth it for a special night out.

I look forward to hearing your thoughts on these options.

Best regards,
Lisa

Choose the best options:

5. Lisa and Alex (work together/are friends/are siblings/are roommates)
6. The main purpose of the dinner is (to celebrate a special occasion/to have a business meeting/to try new cuisines/to meet with friends)
7. Lisa seems (enthusiastic about the options/undecided

about the choices/uninterested in planning/unaware of dietary restrictions)

8. The price for Restaurant A is (expensive/reasonable/affordable/exorbitant).

Answer Key:

1. The price is a bit expensive.
2. We can expect to spend around an hour to two hours there.
3. The price is quite high compared to some other options.
4. The price is a bit steep but could be worth it for a special night out.
5. The main purpose of the dinner is to meet with friends.
6. Lisa and Alex are friends.
7. Lisa seems enthusiastic about the options.
8. The price for Restaurant A is expensive.
9. Restaurant B can be expected to spend around an hour to two hours for the meal.

Practice 3: Part 2: Reading to Apply a Diagram

Read the following diagram:

1. Museum:
- Extensive art collection
- Interactive exhibits
- Guided tours available
- Price: $25 per person
- Duration: 2 hours

2. Zoo:
- Wide variety of animal species
- Educational shows and feeding sessions
- Children's play area
- Price: $18 per person
- Duration: 3 hours

3. Theme Park:
- Thrilling rides and roller coasters
- Live entertainment shows
- Food and beverage outlets
- Price: $60 per person
- Duration: Full day

4. Botanical Gardens:
- Beautiful gardens and landscapes
- Picnic areas and walking trails
- Plant and flower exhibitions
- Price: $10 per person
- Duration: 2 hours"

Read the following email message about the diagram. Complete the email by filling the blanks:

"Subject: Weekend outing
To: Lisa Thompson <lthompson@xxxx.com>
From: Michael Anderson <manderson@xxxx.com>

Hi Lisa,

I hope you're doing well. I wanted to discuss our plans for the weekend. I've been looking at some options for us to enjoy our time off. Here are the choices we have. The museum seems to be the 1. (most desirable) option because of its extensive art collection and interactive exhibits. It would be a great opportunity for us to appreciate art and learn something new. The zoo, on the other hand, offers a wide variety of animal species and educational shows. It's a 2. (fun/educational/scenic/relaxing) option, especially if we're interested in wildlife. Alternatively, we could go to the theme park and experience thrilling rides and live entertainment shows. It might be a bit more expensive, but it promises a full day of excitement. Lastly, the botanical gardens provide a serene environment with beautiful gardens and walking trails. It's a 4. (peaceful/energetic/crowded/bustling) option where we can relax and enjoy nature.

Let me know which option you prefer, or if you have any other ideas.

Best regards,
Michael"

Choose the best options:

5. Michael and Lisa (work together/are friends/are siblings/live in the same neighborhood)
6. The main purpose of the outing is (to celebrate a birthday/to enjoy a weekend/to attend a wedding/to explore a new city)
7. Michael seems (enthusiastic/indifferent/cooperative/indecisive)
8. Based on the information provided, which option offers the longest duration of activity?

Answer Key:

1. most desirable

2. less convenient
3. airport
4. driving
5. go sightseeing
6. are friends
7. to attend a conference
8. cooperative
9. Theme Park

Practice 4: Part 2: Reading to Apply a Diagram

Read the following diagram:

Here's a similar CELPIP Reading Task 2 with a different topic:

"Read the following diagram:

1. Restaurant A:
- Fine dining experience
- Gourmet cuisine
- Reservation recommended
- Price: $150 per person
- Duration: 3 hours

2. Food Truck:
- Quick and casual dining
- Various street food options
- No reservation required
- Price: $10-$15 per item
- Duration: 30 minutes

3. Café:
- Cozy atmosphere
- Coffee and pastries
- No reservation required
- Price: $20 per person
- Duration: 1 hour

4. Buffet:
- All-you-can-eat
- Wide range of international dishes
- No reservation required
- Price: $30 per person
- Duration: 2 hours"

Read the following email message about the diagram. Complete the email by filling the blanks:

"Subject: Dinner plans
To: Sarah Johnson <sjohnson@xxxx.com>
From: David Smith <dsmith@xxxx.com>

Hi Sarah,

I hope this email finds you well. I wanted to discuss our dinner plans for Saturday night. I've been looking at some options for us to enjoy a nice meal. Here are the choices we have. Restaurant A is the 1. (most desirable) option if we want a fine dining experience with gourmet cuisine. It would be a perfect choice for a special occasion. On the other hand, if we're looking for something quick and casual, the food truck offers various street food options. It's 2. (affordable/delicious/popular/quickest), and we won't need to make a reservation. Alternatively, we could go to a cozy café for a relaxing evening. They have coffee and pastries, and no reservation is required. Lastly, there's a buffet where we can enjoy a wide range of international dishes. It's a 4. (budget-friendly/filling/chaotic/extravagant) option for those who love variety.

Let me know which option appeals to you the most, or if you have any other ideas.

Best regards,
David"

Choose the best options:

5. David and Sarah (work together/are friends/are roommates/live in the same city)
6. The main purpose of the dinner is (to celebrate a birthday/to enjoy a casual meal/to discuss business matters/to try international cuisine)
7. David seems (enthusiastic/indifferent/cooperative/indecisive)
8. Based on the information provided, which option offers the longest duration of dining experience? (Restaurant A/Food truck/Cafe/Buffet)

Answer Key:

1. most desirable
2. less convenient
3. airport
4. driving
5. go sightseeing
6. are friends
7. to attend a conference
8. cooperative
9. Restaurant A

Part 3: Reading for Information

The CELPIP Reading Part 3 aims to evaluate your ability to read and understand various types of informational texts commonly encountered in everyday life, workplace settings, or academic contexts.

Format:
In Part 3, you are presented with a series of four to five short texts, such as newspaper articles, advertisements, notices, schedules, or informational brochures. Each text is followed by three to five multiple-choice questions. Candidates must carefully read the texts and choose the best answer option for each question from the given choices.

Types of Texts:
The texts in this section cover a range of topics, including travel, health, lifestyle, education, business, and more. The texts may include descriptions, announcements, instructions, reports, or advertisements. They are designed to mimic real-world situations where the candidate needs to extract specific information from written materials.

Skills Assessed:
CELPIP Reading Part 3 primarily assesses the candidate's ability to:

1. Understand factual information: Candidates must comprehend the main ideas, details, and specific information presented in the texts.
2. Make inferences: Candidates may need to draw conclusions or make logical deductions based on the information provided.
3. Interpret vocabulary and idiomatic expressions: Candidates should understand the meaning of words and phrases used in the texts, including idiomatic expressions.
4. Recognize text organization: Candidates should be able to identify the overall structure of the texts, such as headings,

subheadings, or bullet points, to locate information more efficiently.

5. Evaluate information: Candidates must analyze the texts to determine the accuracy, reliability, or relevance of the information presented.

Strategies:

To succeed in CELPIP Reading Part 3, candidates can employ various strategies, including:

- Skimming the texts to get a general idea of the content and purpose.
- Scanning the texts to locate specific information relevant to each question.
- Paying attention to keywords, dates, numbers, or other cues that may help identify the correct answer.
- Eliminating answer options that are clearly incorrect or do not align with the information in the text.
- Taking note of time management to ensure that all questions are attempted within the given time frame.

Scoring:

Each question in CELPIP Reading Part 3 carries one mark. The section is scored based on the number of correct answers, with no penalty for incorrect responses. The final score is reported on a scale of 1 to 12, with 12 being the highest.

Preparation:

To perform well in CELPIP Reading Part 3, candidates can enhance their skills by practicing reading and comprehending various types of informational texts. This can involve reading newspaper articles, brochures, instruction manuals, or academic texts to develop familiarity with different writing styles and topics. Additionally, candidates can work on improving their vocabulary and comprehension abilities through targeted exercises and practice tests.

By effectively applying reading strategies and practicing with relevant materials, candidates can enhance their performance in CELPIP Reading Part 3: Reading for Information and achieve their desired scores in the test.

15 Tips for Part 3: Reading for Information

Here are 15 tips with strategies and examples to help you pass CELPIP Reading Part 3: Reading for Information:

1. Skim the Passage: Quickly read through the passage to get an overall idea of the content. Pay attention to headings, subheadings, and any highlighted or bolded text.

Example: Skim the passage about renewable energy sources to identify the main topics discussed, such as solar power, wind energy, and hydroelectric power.

2. Identify Keywords: Identify keywords or key phrases in the questions and actively search for them in the passage. This will help you locate relevant information more efficiently.

Example: If the question asks about the benefits of exercise, look for keywords like "benefits," "exercise," or related synonyms in the passage.

3. Highlight Key Information: Use highlighting or underlining to mark important details or key information in the passage. This will make it easier to refer back to specific points when answering questions.

Example: Highlight statistics, dates, or specific examples mentioned in the passage that relate to the main topic or idea.

4. Pay Attention to Signal Words: Look out for signal words or phrases that indicate important information, such as "however," "on the other hand," "in contrast," or "similarly." These words can help you understand the relationship between ideas or arguments.

Example: If the passage discusses advantages and disadvantages, signal words like "pros and cons" or "benefits versus drawbacks" can guide you to the relevant information.

5. Practice Paraphrasing: Develop the skill of paraphrasing by restating information from the passage in your own words. This will help you better understand the content and also aid in answering questions.

Example: If the passage states, "Research shows that lack of sleep can lead to various health problems," you can paraphrase it as "Insufficient sleep has been linked to a range of health issues, according to research."

6. Use Context Clues: Utilize context clues to understand the meaning of unfamiliar words or phrases. Pay attention to the surrounding text for hints about the word's definition.

Example: If you encounter the word "formidable" in the passage, the context may suggest it means "difficult" or "challenging."

7. Practice Predicting: Make predictions about the content or information based on the title, headings, or introductory sentences. This will help you anticipate the main ideas and locate relevant details more effectively.

Example: Before reading a passage titled "The Benefits of Meditation," predict that it will discuss advantages like stress reduction, improved focus, and mental clarity.

8. Analyze Graphs and Charts: If the passage includes graphs, charts, or tables, carefully analyze the data presented. Look for trends, patterns, or comparisons to answer questions related to the visual representation.

Example: Analyze a bar graph that shows the percentage of students studying different subjects to answer a question about the most popular field of study.

9. Practice Time Management: Allocate a specific amount of time to each passage and its associated questions. Be mindful of the time remaining and adjust your pace accordingly to ensure you have enough time to answer all questions.

Example: Set a target time of 8 minutes to read the passage and 2 minutes to answer each question. This will help you stay on track and complete the section within the given time limit.

10. Read All Answer Choices: Carefully read all answer choices before selecting the best option. Sometimes, a seemingly correct answer can be eliminated by considering all the choices.

Example: If the question asks for the main purpose of the passage, read all the answer choices to ensure you choose the one that best aligns with the overall theme or objective.

11. Check for Consistency: Ensure that your selected answer choice aligns with the information provided in the passage. Double-check if the choice contradicts any statements or if there is evidence to support it.

Example: If the passage clearly states that a particular theory has been debunked, make sure your selected answer does not support that theory.

12. Pay Attention to Detail: Read the questions and answer choices carefully, paying attention to small details or specific qualifiers. Missing or misinterpreting these details can lead to incorrect answers.

Example: If the question asks for the "most common" reason, ensure your chosen answer reflects the highest occurrence among the options provided.

13. Eliminate Distraction Choices: Use the process of elimination to eliminate answer choices that are clearly incorrect or irrelevant. This increases your chances of selecting the correct answer from the remaining choices.

Example: If the question asks for the cause of a specific event, eliminate answer choices that discuss unrelated effects or outcomes.

14. Review Your Answers: If time allows, review your answers before submitting the test. Check for any errors or inconsistencies that you may have missed initially.

Example: Go back to the passage and re-read the relevant sections to confirm your selected answers and ensure they are supported by the information provided.

15. Practice Regularly: Regular practice is essential for improving your reading skills and becoming familiar with the CELPIP format. Set aside dedicated study time to work on reading comprehension and answering practice questions.

Example: Use online resources or study guides to access sample passages and questions similar to those in the CELPIP test. Practice regularly to build confidence and enhance your performance.

By following these strategies and utilizing the provided examples, you can develop effective reading strategies and increase your chances of success in CELPIP Reading Part 3: Reading for Information. Remember to practice consistently, manage your time wisely, and stay focused during the test.

Practice 1: Part 3: Reading for Information

Read the following passage:

A. Coffee is one of the most popular beverages in the world, consumed by millions of people on a daily basis. It is derived from the roasted seeds of the Coffea plant, which is native to tropical regions of Africa. The cultivation of coffee has expanded to various parts of the world, including South America, Central America, and Asia. The drink is known for its distinct flavor and its ability to provide a stimulating effect due to the presence of caffeine.

B. There are several different types of coffee beans, each with its own unique characteristics. Arabica and Robusta are the two most common varieties. Arabica beans are generally considered to be of higher quality, producing a smoother and more flavorful cup of coffee. Robusta beans, on the other hand, are known for their higher caffeine content and stronger taste. Coffee enthusiasts often have their preferences when it comes to the type of beans used in their brew.

C. The process of preparing coffee involves several steps. First, the coffee beans are harvested and then processed to remove the outer layers. The beans are then roasted to bring out their flavors and aromas. Once roasted, the beans are ground into a fine powder, which is then brewed with hot water. The brewing methods can vary, with popular options including drip brewing, espresso, and French press. The final result is a flavorful and energizing beverage enjoyed by coffee lovers around the world.

D. Coffee has a rich cultural and social history. It has been a part of various traditions and rituals in different societies. Coffeehouses have often served as meeting places for intellectuals, artists, and thinkers, fostering the exchange of ideas and discussions. In some cultures, coffee ceremonies are held to honor guests or mark special occasions. Additionally, coffee has become a significant part of modern lifestyle, with coffee shops and specialty cafes flourishing in many cities, offering a wide range of coffee varieties and preparations.

E. Not given in any of the above paragraphs.

Decide which paragraph, A to D, has the information given in each statement below. Select E if the information is not given in any of the paragraphs:

1. The Coffea plant is native to Africa. (A/B/C/D/E)
2. Arabica beans are known for their smoother flavor. (A/B/C/D/E)
3. Coffee undergoes a series of processing steps before it is brewed. (A/B/C/D/E)
4. Coffee has played a role in cultural and social activities throughout history. (A/B/C/D/E)
5. There are different types of coffee brewing methods. (A/B/C/D/E)
6. Coffee consumption is a global phenomenon. (A/B/C/D/E)
7. Coffeehouses have served as venues for intellectual discussions. (A/B/C/D/E)
8. Coffee ceremonies are practiced in various cultures. (A/B/C/D/E)
9. Coffee shops offer a wide range of coffee options. (A/B/C/D/E)

Answer Key:

1. A
2. B
3. C
4. D
5. C
6. A
7. D
8. D
9. D

Practice 2: Part 3: Reading for Information

Read the following passage:

A. Orchids are a diverse group of flowering plants that belong to the family Orchidaceae. They are known for their intricate and often brightly colored blooms, which come in a wide range of shapes and sizes. Orchids can be found in various habitats around the world, including tropical rainforests, deserts, and even Arctic tundra. With over 25,000 known species, orchids are among the largest families of flowering plants.

B. One of the remarkable features of orchids is their ability to attract pollinators through adaptations in their flowers. Many orchids have evolved unique strategies to entice specific pollinators, such as bees, moths, butterflies, or birds. These strategies include producing fragrant scents, mimicking the appearance of female insects, or offering nectar as a reward. By attracting pollinators, orchids ensure successful pollination and subsequent seed production.

C. Orchid cultivation has been a popular hobby for enthusiasts around the world. Growing orchids can be challenging due to their specific requirements, including proper humidity, temperature, light levels, and air circulation. Hobbyists often create specialized environments, such as greenhouses or terrariums, to provide optimal conditions for their orchid collections. Orchid shows and exhibitions are held globally, showcasing the beauty and diversity of these fascinating plants.

D. Orchids have long held cultural significance in various societies. In many ancient civilizations, orchids were associated with fertility, love, and beauty. They were often used in traditional medicine for their perceived healing properties. Additionally, orchids have been sought after by collectors and traded as valuable commodities throughout history. Today, they continue to be highly valued in the floral industry, with exotic orchid varieties often commanding high prices.

E. Not given in any of the above paragraphs.

Decide which paragraph, A to D, has the information given in each statement below. Select E if the information is not given in any of the paragraphs:

1. There are different types of orchids found in diverse habitats. (A/B/C/D/E)
2. Orchids use various adaptations to attract pollinators. (A/B/C/D/E)
3. Orchid cultivation can be challenging due to specific requirements. (A/B/C/D/E)
4. Orchids have historical and cultural significance. (A/B/C/D/E)
5. Orchid enthusiasts showcase their plants at exhibitions. (A/B/C/D/E)
6. Orchids have been used in traditional medicine. (A/B/C/D/E)
7. Orchids are traded as valuable commodities. (A/B/C/D/E)
8. Orchids are known for their delicate and vibrant blooms. (A/B/C/D/E)
9. Orchids are exclusively found in tropical rainforests. (A/B/C/D/E)

Answer Key:

1. A
2. B
3. C
4. D
5. C
6. D
7. D
8. A
9. E

Practice 3: Part 3: Reading for Information

Read the following passage:

A. The pangolin is a unique mammal found in parts of Africa and Asia. There are eight species of pangolins, all of which are endangered due to illegal hunting and trafficking. Pangolins are known for their unique scales, which are made of keratin and provide protection against predators. These scales are highly sought after in some countries for their supposed medicinal properties. Pangolins have long tongues that can extend up to 40 centimeters, which they use to eat ants and termites.

B. The diet of pangolins consists primarily of insects. They have specialized adaptations to facilitate their feeding habits. Pangolins lack teeth and instead use their strong stomach muscles and gizzard to grind up food. They have a highly efficient digestive system that allows them to extract nutrients from their insect diet. Pangolins are also known for their ability to consume a large number of ants and termites in a single night.

C. Pangolins have a unique defense mechanism against predators. When threatened, they will roll up into a tight ball, protecting their vulnerable belly and exposing their sharp scales. This makes it difficult for predators to attack them. Additionally, pangolins can emit a strong-smelling secretion from their anal glands as a defensive mechanism. This pungent odor helps ward off potential threats.

D. The trade of pangolins and their body parts is a major concern for conservationists. Their scales are highly valued in traditional medicine practices, particularly in some Asian countries. Despite international regulations and efforts to curb the illegal trade, pangolins continue to be poached and trafficked. The demand for pangolins has put significant pressure on their populations, leading to a decline in their numbers. Conservation organizations are working to raise awareness and implement measures to protect these unique mammals.

E. Not given in any of the above paragraphs."

Decide which paragraph, A to D, has the information given in each statement below. Select E if the information is not given in any of the paragraphs:

1. Pangolins have specialized adaptations for their feeding habits. (A/B/C/D/E)
2. Pangolins are hunted for their scales. (A/B/C/D/E)
3. Pangolins can emit a strong odor as a defense mechanism. (A/B/C/D/E)
4. The trade of pangolins is a major conservation concern. (A/B/C/D/E)
5. Pangolins are known for their ability to eat a large number of ants and termites. (A/B/C/D/E)
6. There are efforts to protect pangolins from illegal trade. (A/B/C/D/E)
7. Pangolins are native to both Africa and Asia. (A/B/C/D/E)
8. Pangolins have teeth for chewing their food. (A/B/C/D/E)
9. The population of pangolins is stable and not at risk. (A/B/C/D/E)

Answer Key:

1. A
2. A
3. C
4. D
5. A
6. D
7. A
8. E
9. E

Practice 4: Part 3: Reading for Information

Read the following passage:

A. The koala is a unique marsupial native to Australia. Known for its adorable appearance, it is often referred to as a "koala bear," although it is not a bear at all. Koalas are primarily found in eucalyptus forests along the eastern coast of Australia. They have a distinct diet consisting almost entirely of eucalyptus leaves, which provide them with both nutrition and hydration.

B. Koalas are well adapted to their arboreal lifestyle. They have sharp claws and strong limbs that allow them to climb trees with ease. Their large, furry ears provide excellent hearing, while their keen sense of smell helps them locate the most nutritious eucalyptus leaves. Koalas spend most of their time perched in trees, where they sleep, rest, and feed.

C. The koala's diet of eucalyptus leaves poses some challenges. Eucalyptus leaves are tough and fibrous, containing toxins that are harmful to many other animals. However, koalas have a specialized digestive system that enables them to break down these toxins and extract nutrients from the leaves. They have a long digestive tract and a slow metabolic rate, allowing them to efficiently process their food.

D. Koala populations have been declining in recent years due to various factors. Habitat loss, primarily caused by deforestation and urbanization, has severely impacted koala numbers. The fragmentation of their habitat has disrupted their movement and breeding patterns. Additionally, diseases such as chlamydia and bushfires have also taken a toll on koala populations.

E. Not given in any of the above paragraphs."

Decide which paragraph, A to D, has the information given in each statement below. Select E if the information is not given in any of the paragraphs:

1. Koalas primarily feed on eucalyptus leaves. (A/B/C/D/E)
2. Koalas have adaptations that help them climb trees. (A/B/C/D/E)
3. The koala's digestive system allows it to process toxins in eucalyptus leaves. (A/B/C/D/E)
4. Koala populations have been declining due to various factors. (A/B/C/D/E)
5. Koalas are often mistaken for being a type of bear. (A/B/C/D/E)
6. Koalas have a fast metabolic rate. (A/B/C/D/E)
7. Diseases and bushfires have affected koala populations. (A/B/C/D/E)
8. Koalas are found in different habitats across Australia. (A/B/C/D/E)
9. Koalas rely on their excellent eyesight to locate food. (A/B/C/D/E)

Answer Key:

1. A
2. B
3. C
4. D
5. A
6. E
7. D
8. A
9. E

Part 4: Reading for Viewpoints

Part 4 of the CELPIP Reading section focuses on reading for viewpoints. This part assesses your understanding of different perspectives, opinions, and attitudes expressed in a variety of written materials, such as newspaper articles, blog posts, opinion pieces, and essays. The main objective of this part is to gauge the test taker's ability to comprehend and analyze texts from different viewpoints.

Here is a detailed overview of the CELPIP Reading Part 4:

1. Format: The Reading Part 4 section consists of several short texts, usually three or four in number. Each text is followed by a set of multiple-choice questions. The texts are typically around 100-150 words in length, and the questions assess the test taker's ability to identify viewpoints, opinions, arguments, and the main idea of each text.

2. Reading Skills Assessed: This section assesses several important reading skills, including:
- Comprehension: Understanding the main ideas and supporting details in the texts.
- Inference: Making logical deductions based on the information presented.
- Analysis: Identifying the author's viewpoint and purpose.
- Critical Thinking: Evaluating arguments, opinions, and perspectives presented in the texts.

3. Types of Questions: The questions in Part 4 of the Reading section can vary, but they generally fall into the following categories:
- Identifying the main idea: Test takers are required to determine the primary focus or purpose of the text.
- Identifying viewpoints: Test takers must recognize the author's perspective or opinion on a particular issue.
- Recognizing supporting details: Test takers need to identify

statements or evidence that support the author's viewpoint.
- Making inferences: Test takers are asked to draw logical conclusions based on the information provided in the text.
- Analyzing arguments: Test takers evaluate the strength or weakness of arguments presented in the text.

4. Strategies for Success:
- Skim the text: Quickly read through the text to get a general understanding of the topic and the author's perspective.
- Read the questions first: Before reading the text in detail, read the questions to know what to look for while reading.
- Identify keywords: Pay attention to keywords and phrases that indicate the author's viewpoint or opinion.
- Take notes: Jot down key points, arguments, or any information that helps you understand the author's perspective.
- Eliminate incorrect options: Use the process of elimination to narrow down the answer choices and increase your chances of selecting the correct answer.

5. Time Management: It is essential to manage your time effectively in this section. Allocate sufficient time to read and analyze each text, and be mindful of the time available to answer the questions.

6. Practice: To excel in Part 4 of the CELPIP Reading section, practice reading various types of texts from different viewpoints. This will help you become familiar with different writing styles, improve your comprehension skills, and enhance your ability to identify viewpoints effectively.

In conclusion, Part 4 of the CELPIP Reading section, "Reading for Viewpoints," tests your ability to understand and analyze different perspectives, opinions, and attitudes presented in short texts. By developing strong reading comprehension skills, analyzing arguments, and recognizing viewpoints, you can improve your performance in this section of the CELPIP test.

10 Tips for Part 4: Reading for Viewpoints

Here are 15 tips, strategies, and examples to help you succeed in CELPIP Reading Part 4: Reading for Viewpoints:

1. Read the Passage Thoroughly: Take your time to read the entire passage carefully. Pay attention to the author's arguments, supporting evidence, and any contrasting viewpoints presented.

Example: Read the following passage excerpt:
"Many people argue that video games are detrimental to children's development, citing increased aggression and decreased academic performance as evidence. However, recent studies have shown that video games can enhance problem-solving skills and improve hand-eye coordination."

2. Identify the Main Idea: Determine the central point or main idea of the passage. This will help you understand the author's viewpoint and guide you in answering related questions.

Example: The main idea of the passage is that there are differing opinions on the impact of video games on children's development.

3. Analyze Tone and Language: Pay attention to the author's tone and language choices. This can provide insights into their perspective and help you identify any biases or persuasive techniques used.

Example: The author uses neutral language to present contrasting viewpoints, indicating an objective approach.

4. Recognize Implicit Viewpoints: Look for viewpoints that are implied rather than explicitly stated. Consider the overall message and the author's underlying assumptions.

Example: Although not directly stated, the author's positive language and emphasis on recent studies suggest a favorable viewpoint towards video games.

5. Identify Supporting Evidence: Take note of any evidence or examples provided by the author to support their viewpoint. This will help you understand the strength of their arguments.

Example: The passage mentions recent studies that demonstrate the positive effects of video games on problem-solving skills and hand-eye coordination.

6. Consider Counterarguments: Be aware of counterarguments or opposing viewpoints that may be presented in the passage. This will help you analyze the author's stance more critically.

Example: The author may acknowledge the argument about the negative impact of video games on academic performance but offer contrasting evidence to support their viewpoint.

7. Pay Attention to Transitions: Look for transition words or phrases that indicate shifts in viewpoint or the presentation of alternative perspectives.

Example: Transition words such as "however," "on the other hand," or "in contrast" can signal the introduction of a different viewpoint.

8. Infer the Author's Purpose: Consider the author's purpose in presenting the viewpoints. Are they attempting to persuade, inform, or present a balanced argument? Understanding the purpose can guide your interpretation of the passage.

Example: The author may aim to present a balanced argument by acknowledging both positive and negative viewpoints on video games.

9. Evaluate Bias and Assumptions: Be mindful of any biases or assumptions that the author may have. Look for evidence that supports or challenges their perspective.

Example: If the author consistently cites studies funded by video game companies, it may indicate a potential bias.

10. Review Answer Choices: Carefully analyze each answer choice before making a selection. Look for options that align with the author's viewpoint, considering the tone, language, and evidence presented in the passage.

Example: If the passage emphasizes the benefits of video games, select an answer choice that reflects a positive viewpoint.

11. Eliminate Distractors: Eliminate answer choices that are clearly inconsistent with the passage or go against the author's viewpoint. Cross out options that are extreme or unrelated to the arguments presented.

Example: If the passage focuses on the positive effects of video games, eliminate answer choices that only discuss the negative aspects.

12. Consider Context: Consider the broader context of the passage and the topic being discussed. This can help you understand the significance of the viewpoints and the relevance of the arguments presented.

Example: If the passage is about the impact of video games on children, consider how societal factors and developmental stages may influence the perspectives.

13. Use Prior Knowledge: Utilize your prior knowledge and personal experiences to analyze the viewpoints presented. Relate the arguments to real-life situations or examples you are familiar with.

Example: If the passage discusses the benefits of exercise, relate it to your own experiences of feeling more energized and focused after physical activity.

14. Practice Active Reading: Engage in active reading techniques such as underlining key points, jotting down notes, or summarizing each viewpoint. This will help you internalize the information and better remember the details.

Example: Summarize each viewpoint in a few words or phrases to help clarify your understanding of the passage.

15. Time Management: Allocate your time wisely. Skim the passage initially to understand its main ideas, then focus on reading in-depth and answering questions. Avoid spending too much time on a single question, as there are multiple passages to complete within the given time.

Example: Set a time limit for each passage and question to ensure you have enough time to complete the entire section.

Remember to practice these strategies with sample passages and questions to improve your skills and familiarity with the CELPIP Reading Part 4 format.

Practice 1: Part 4: Reading for Viewpoints

Read the following article from a website:

For decades, traditional farming methods have dominated the agricultural landscape, but now a new trend is emerging: urban farming. Urban farming refers to the practice of growing crops and raising animals in urban areas, such as rooftops, balconies, and vacant lots. This innovative approach to agriculture is gaining popularity for several reasons.

One of the main reasons for the rise of urban farming is the increasing concern over food security. As urban populations continue to grow, there is a greater demand for locally grown, fresh produce. Urban farming allows communities to become more self-sufficient in their food production, reducing their dependence on distant farms and the associated transportation costs. By growing food in the heart of the city, urban farmers can provide residents with access to nutritious, organic produce.

Another benefit of urban farming is its positive impact on the environment. Traditional farming practices often involve the use of chemical fertilizers, pesticides, and large amounts of water. In contrast, urban farmers tend to utilize organic methods and employ sustainable techniques such as composting and rainwater harvesting. By adopting these practices, urban farming helps to reduce the carbon footprint associated with food production and promotes a healthier ecosystem within the city.

Furthermore, urban farming has significant social and economic advantages. It can serve as a catalyst for community engagement and empowerment. Residents, regardless of age or background, can participate in the farming process, fostering a sense of belonging and pride in their neighborhood. Additionally, urban farming can create job opportunities and stimulate local economies. Farmers' markets and farm-to-table initiatives provide avenues for urban farmers to sell their products directly to consumers, creating a sustainable source of income for individuals and contributing to the local economy.

While urban farming presents many opportunities, there are also challenges that need to be addressed. Limited space, access to resources, and potential conflicts with zoning regulations are some of the hurdles urban farmers face. However, with proper planning, supportive policies, and community collaboration, these challenges can be overcome, paving the way for a thriving urban farming movement.

Choose the best option according to the information given on the website:

1. This article is about ....
A) the benefits and challenges of urban farming
B) the rise of organic farming practices in rural areas
C) the history and evolution of traditional farming methods
D) the impact of urbanization on the agricultural landscape

2. Urban farming is gaining popularity due to ....
A) the need for affordable housing in urban areas
B) the desire for locally grown, fresh produce
C) the implementation of large-scale agricultural projects
D) the decline of traditional farming practices

3. Urban farming contributes to a healthier environment by ....
A) utilizing chemical fertilizers and pesticides
B) promoting the use of large amounts of water
C) reducing the carbon footprint of food production
D) relying on distant farms for food supply

4. One of the social benefits of urban farming is ....
A) the creation of job opportunities for urban residents
B) the increase in food prices in urban areas
C) the dependency on imported produce
D) the reliance on large-scale farming corporations

5. Urban farming faces challenges such as ....
A) limited space and access to resources
B) high demand for locally grown produce
C) the lack of community engagement and empowerment
D) the absence of supportive policies for farming initiatives

The following is a comment by a visitor to the website page. Complete the comment by choosing the best option to fill in each blank.

Great article! As an urban dweller, _6.(I am skeptical about the feasibility of urban farming/I have always been interested in organic farming/I believe traditional farming methods are more effective/ I have witnessed the benefits of urban farming)_ firsthand. The availability of fresh produce within the city limits is a game-changer. Not only does it promote healthier eating habits, but it also reduces our reliance on long-distance transportation. I've noticed that _7.(urban farming often leads to higher food prices/ urban farmers prioritize sustainability over profit/urban farming helps build stronger communities/urban farmers face difficulties due to zoning regulations)_, as it brings people together and fosters a sense of community. Additionally, I believe that _8.(urban farming can create job opportunities/urban farming is limited to small-scale operations/urban farming is detrimental to the environment/urban farming relies heavily on chemical inputs)_ with proper support and planning, urban farming has the potential to transform our cities and make them more sustainable. It's time we embrace this innovative approach to agriculture and reap its numerous benefits.

Answer Key:

1) A) the benefits and challenges of urban farming
2) B) the desire for locally grown, fresh produce
3) C) reducing the carbon footprint of food production
4) C) the dependency on imported produce
5) A) limited space and access to resources

6) I have witnessed the benefits of urban farming
7) Urban farming helps build stronger communities
8) Urban farming can create job opportunities.

Practice 2: Part 4: Reading for Viewpoints

Read the following article from a website:

The Benefits of Bilingual Education

Bilingual education has been a subject of discussion and debate in the field of education for many years. With an increasingly globalized world, the advantages of being fluent in multiple languages are becoming more apparent. Bilingual education programs aim to provide students with the opportunity to become proficient in two or more languages while gaining a deep understanding of different cultures.

One of the key benefits of bilingual education is enhanced cognitive skills. Research has shown that bilingual individuals have better problem-solving abilities, improved memory, and greater mental flexibility compared to monolingual individuals. The constant practice of switching between languages strengthens the brain's executive functions, leading to improved cognitive abilities.

Bilingual education also fosters cultural appreciation and understanding. By learning a second language, students gain insights into different customs, traditions, and perspectives. This exposure promotes tolerance, empathy, and a broader worldview. Bilingual individuals are more likely to appreciate diversity and engage in cross-cultural communication, which are crucial skills in our interconnected world.

Furthermore, bilingual education provides long-term career advantages. In today's global economy, many employers value candidates who can communicate effectively with international clients and colleagues. Bilingual individuals have a competitive edge in the job market, as they can bridge language and cultural gaps, opening doors to a wider range of career opportunities.

Despite the numerous benefits, some skeptics argue that bilingual education may hinder academic progress in other subjects. However, studies have shown that bilingual students perform just as well, if not better, in core subjects like mathematics and science compared to their monolingual peers. In fact, bilingualism can enhance overall academic performance, as the cognitive skills developed through language acquisition transfer to other areas of learning.

In conclusion, bilingual education offers a range of advantages for students. It enhances cognitive abilities, promotes cultural understanding, and provides career opportunities. Contrary to common misconceptions, bilingualism does not hinder academic progress but rather supports it. Embracing bilingual education prepares students for success in an increasingly interconnected and diverse world.

Choose the best option according to the information given on the website:

1. This article is about ....
A) the advantages of bilingual education
B) the challenges of implementing bilingual education
C) the controversy surrounding bilingual education
D) the impact of globalization on education

2. One of the benefits of bilingual education is ....
A) improved cognitive abilities
B) a narrower worldview
C) limited career options
D) decreased academic performance

3. Bilingual education promotes cultural appreciation and understanding by ....
A) limiting exposure to different customs and perspectives
B) discouraging empathy and tolerance
C) fostering cross-cultural communication
D) focusing solely on language acquisition

4. According to the article, bilingual individuals have an advantage in the job market because they can ....
A) engage in monolingual communication
B) bridge language and cultural gaps
C) limit their career opportunities
D) excel only in international companies

5. Studies have shown that bilingual students ....
A) perform worse than monolingual students in core subjects
B) struggle with cognitive abilities and memory
C) have limited career opportunities
D) perform as well as or better than monolingual students in core subjects

The following is a comment by a visitor to the website page. Complete the comment by choosing the best option to fill in each blank.

Great article! As an educator with many years of experience, _6. (I have witnessed the benefits of bilingual education/I believe monolingualism is superior/I find the disadvantages of bilingual education outweigh the advantages/I have encountered challenges in implementing bilingual programs)._ The cognitive benefits of bilingualism are undeniable. I have seen students develop sharper problem-solving skills and improved memory through language acquisition. Moreover, bilingual education promotes _7. (intolerance and cultural misunderstandings/cross-cultural understanding and empathy/limited worldview and perspective/ open-mindedness and diversity)._ Students who learn another language gain a deeper understanding of different cultures, and this understanding helps create a more inclusive society. Additionally, bilingualism provides _8. (limited career options/a competitive edge in the job market/narrow professional prospects/ a disadvantage in employment)._ In today's globalized world, employers highly value individuals who can communicate effectively with diverse groups. Finally, it's important to debunk the misconception that bilingual education hinders academic progress. In my experience, *9. (bilingual students perform just as well as monolingual students/bilingualism negatively affects academic performance/bilingual education focuses solely on language acquisition/bilingualism limits cognitive development).* Bilingual students excel not only in language skills but also in other academic subjects. Overall, I strongly believe in the power and benefits of bilingual education for students.

Answer Key:

1. A) the advantages of bilingual education
2. A) improved cognitive abilities
3. C) fostering cross-cultural communication
4. B) bridge language and cultural gaps
5. D) perform as well as or better than monolingual students in core subjects
6. I have witnessed the benefits of bilingual education.
7. Cross-cultural understanding and empathy.
8. A competitive edge in the job market.
9. Bilingual students perform just as well as monolingual students.

Practice 3: Part 4: Reading for Viewpoints

Read the following article from a website:

Many people dream of starting their own business and becoming their own boss. However, for most, it remains just a dream. One entrepreneur, Lisa Martinez, decided to turn her dream into a reality and founded a unique business that combines two popular passions: coffee and books.

Martinez opened "Coffee & Chapters," a cozy café that offers customers the opportunity to enjoy a good book while sipping on a delicious cup of coffee. The concept emerged from Martinez's own love for both reading and coffee. She believed that the two could create a delightful and relaxing experience for customers.

The café is designed to resemble a cozy library, with bookshelves lining the walls and comfortable seating areas. Customers can browse through a wide selection of books while savoring their coffee. Martinez carefully curates the collection, ensuring a diverse range of genres to cater to different reading preferences.

The idea behind "Coffee & Chapters" goes beyond simply providing a space for reading and enjoying coffee. Martinez believes that the combination of these two activities can foster a sense of community and intellectual stimulation. The café hosts book clubs, author meet-ups, and literary events, creating a vibrant literary scene in the local community.

Despite initial skepticism from some, "Coffee & Chapters" has gained popularity and positive reviews from customers. Many people appreciate the tranquil atmosphere and the opportunity to disconnect from the outside world while immersing themselves in a good book. The café has become a go-to destination for book lovers and coffee enthusiasts alike.

Choose the best option according to the information given on the website:

1. This article is about ....
A) a unique café that combines coffee and books
B) the benefits of reading and coffee for relaxation
C) the challenges of starting a business as an entrepreneur
D) the popularity of coffee shops in the local community

2. The founder of "Coffee & Chapters," Lisa Martinez, was inspired by her love for ....
A) cooking and baking
B) music and art
C) reading and coffee
D) socializing and networking

3. The café's atmosphere is designed to resemble a ....
A) vibrant community center
B) modern office space
C) cozy library
D) busy coffee shop

4. According to the article, "Coffee & Chapters" fosters a sense of community by hosting ......
A) book clubs and literary events
B) coffee tasting sessions
C) art exhibitions and workshops
D) business networking events

5. The café has gained popularity due to its offering of ....
A) exclusive membership benefits
B) discounted coffee and book bundles
C) free Wi-Fi and workspace facilities
D) a unique combination of reading and coffee

The following is a comment by a visitor to the website page. Complete the comment by choosing the best option to fill in each blank.

Interesting article! I've been an avid reader for years, and I must say that the concept of "Coffee & Chapters" is quite appealing.

It's wonderful to have a dedicated space where _6.(book lovers can connect with fellow readers/entrepreneurs can showcase their business ideas/artists can exhibit their artwork/students can study for exams)_ while enjoying a cup of coffee. It's often difficult to find such places that offer both a relaxing atmosphere and quality coffee. I also appreciate the café's efforts to organize _7. (book signings and poetry readings/live music performances and comedy shows/food tasting events and cooking workshops/business seminars and networking sessions)._ This adds a dynamic element to the café experience and creates opportunities for literary engagement. In my opinion, "Coffee & Chapters" has successfully combined two beloved activities to create a haven for _8.(creatives and thinkers/fitness enthusiasts and health-conscious individuals/ business professionals and entrepreneurs/students and educators)._ It's a refreshing concept that I hope continues to thrive in our community."

Answer Key:

AHere are the correct answers to the questions:

1. A) a unique café that combines coffee and books
2. C) reading and coffee
3. C) cozy library
4. A) book clubs and literary events
5. D) a unique combination of reading and coffee
6. book lovers can connect with fellow readers
7. book signings and poetry readings
8. business professionals and entrepreneurs

Practice 4: Part 4: Reading for Viewpoints

Read the following article from a website:

In recent years, many schools have been embracing the benefits of outdoor education. One particular school, Greenfield Elementary, has taken it to the next level by integrating nature into their daily curriculum.

At Greenfield Elementary, students don't just learn about science and biology from textbooks; they experience it firsthand in their very own outdoor classroom. The school's courtyard has been transformed into a vibrant learning space with garden beds, wildlife habitats, and even a weather station.

The idea behind this initiative is to provide students with a holistic education that connects them with nature and fosters a deeper understanding of the environment. Research has shown that spending time in nature improves cognitive function, creativity, and overall well-being.

The outdoor classroom has become a hub for various educational activities. Students engage in hands-on gardening, learning about plant life cycles and sustainable practices. They observe local wildlife and study their habitats, gaining knowledge about biodiversity and ecosystems. They also learn about weather patterns by collecting data from the weather station and analyzing it in their science classes.

The impact of the outdoor classroom has been remarkable. Teachers have noticed an increase in student engagement and enthusiasm for learning. Students have developed a sense of responsibility towards the environment and have become more mindful of their ecological footprint. Additionally, the outdoor classroom has provided opportunities for cross-curricular integration, where subjects like math and art are incorporated into outdoor activities.

The success of Greenfield Elementary's outdoor classroom has caught the attention of educators nationwide. Many schools are now considering similar initiatives to enhance their students' learning experiences.

Choose the best option according to the information given on the website:

1. This article is about...
A) a school that promotes outdoor education
B) a science experiment conducted at Greenfield Elementary
C) the benefits of traditional classroom settings
D) a weather station used for forecasting

2. The purpose of the outdoor classroom at Greenfield Elementary is to...
A) replace traditional classrooms with an outdoor setting
B) provide students with a break from their regular curriculum
C) connect students with nature and enhance their education
D) conduct experiments related to plant life and wildlife

3. The outdoor classroom at Greenfield Elementary includes...
A) textbooks and traditional teaching methods
B) a dedicated space for physical education activities
C) garden beds, wildlife habitats, and a weather station
D) resources for art and creative expression

4. According to research, spending time in nature can...
A) hinder cognitive function and creativity
B) lead to a decline in overall well-being
C) have a negative impact on student engagement
D) improve cognitive function, creativity, and well-being

5. The impact of the outdoor classroom at Greenfield Elementary includes...
A) a decrease in student engagement and enthusiasm for learning
B) limited opportunities for cross-curricular integration
C) an increase in student responsibility towards the environment

D) a decline in students' understanding of plant life cycles

The following is a comment by a visitor to the website page. Complete the comment by choosing the best option to fill in each blank.

Great article! As an educator myself, I've always believed in the importance of 6. (outdoor education/incorporating technology into classrooms/providing more standardized tests/ strict discipline policies). It's fascinating to see how Greenfield Elementary has successfully implemented an outdoor classroom. While some may argue that students need a traditional classroom setting, research has shown that spending time in nature can 7. (negatively impact cognitive function/boost creativity and overall well-being/improve standardized test scores/limit cross-curricular opportunities). I have witnessed firsthand how outdoor activities can spark a sense of wonder and curiosity among students. They not only learn about the environment but also develop important life skills like problem-solving and teamwork. Additionally, the outdoor classroom allows for a seamless integration of different subjects, creating a well-rounded educational experience. I hope more schools follow in Greenfield Elementary's footsteps and prioritize nature-based learning. It truly makes a difference in students' lives.

Answer Key:

1. A) a school that promotes outdoor education
2. C) connect students with nature and enhance their education
3. C) garden beds, wildlife habitats, and a weather station
4. D) improve cognitive function, creativity, and well-being
5. C) an increase in student responsibility towards the environment
6. A) outdoor education
7. B) boost creativity and overall well-being